Virtue Seeds

This book is dedicated
to our mother
Monique
Mottahedeh

By Elaheh Bos
Colouring pages by Soraya Tohidi

www.plantlovegrow.com
©Plantlovegrow 2016
©Elaheh Bos 2016
Colouring pages © Soraya Tohidi 2016
www.sorayatohidi.com

ISBN: 978-0-9810556-1-9

Legal Deposit, Library and Archives
Canada, 2016

Table of Contents

plant
love
grow

How to use the Virtue Activity Guide

This guide was created as a tool to help teach virtues through group activities, crafts, colouring pages, stories and games. These activities provide learning and discussion opportunities between parents, children, and educators.

Quotes:

Special space has been provided for inspirational quotes. These can be religious, spiritual, scientific, or beautiful sayings that you create to focus your energy on the virtue you are exploring. These quotes can be memorized and are there to provide inspiration.

What you need in your tool box:

- Paper towels.
- Glue (appropriate to age, glue stick is often the easiest).
- Craft paper, magazines, recycled paper, white papers for drawing.
- Scissors (age appropriate).
- Pencil, crayons or markers (what I call colouring or drawing tools).
- Paint and paintbrushes.
- A box full of things you would normally recycle.
- Copies of the activity and colouring pages (enough for everyone).

We suggest giving each child a binder for them to keep their finished projects or to write about the activities. Ask them to personalize their binders.

Before starting any activity:

1. Discuss together three to five simple guidelines for the group to follow during the activities. These guidelines should be inspired by virtues and should focus on the desired behaviour.

2. Preparation is key. Choose the activity ahead of time and prepare your materials. Prepare your space. If you plan on using the virtue guide as part of a scheduled class, read all the activities ahead and add them to your calendar. Always make extra copies of the material you plan to use.

3. Create a routine around the activities. If you do them on a daily basis, arrange a specific time each day. If you do them on a weekly basis, do them on the same day if possible. Everyone will begin to anticipate the next activity with excitement.

4. Create roles and responsibilities to match the age of the children. This will be a great opportunity for them to learn responsibility, and will allow everyone to be involved and feel responsible for the success of the activity.

5. Focus on the process, not the outcome. Learning, spending time together, discussing what a virtue means to us, sharing our own stories and trying something new is more important than the results of an activity. Enjoy the process and discussions.

1. Caring

One way to explain Caring:

Caring is how we show our love for the people and things we cherish. When you care for someone or something you try to help them and you do things to show that these people and things are important to you.

You can care for family, friends, animals, or something special that you own. When you care for something you make sure that it doesn't get damaged. You care for someone by giving them love and respect.

A beautiful quote about Caring:

Write down a quote that you wish to memorize or remember.
If you cannot find a quote to inspire you, try coming up with your own.

Colouring page: See page 61

Talk about the drawing:

> What did Valentine make to show her friend how much she cares for her?

> What can you do to show someone you care for them?

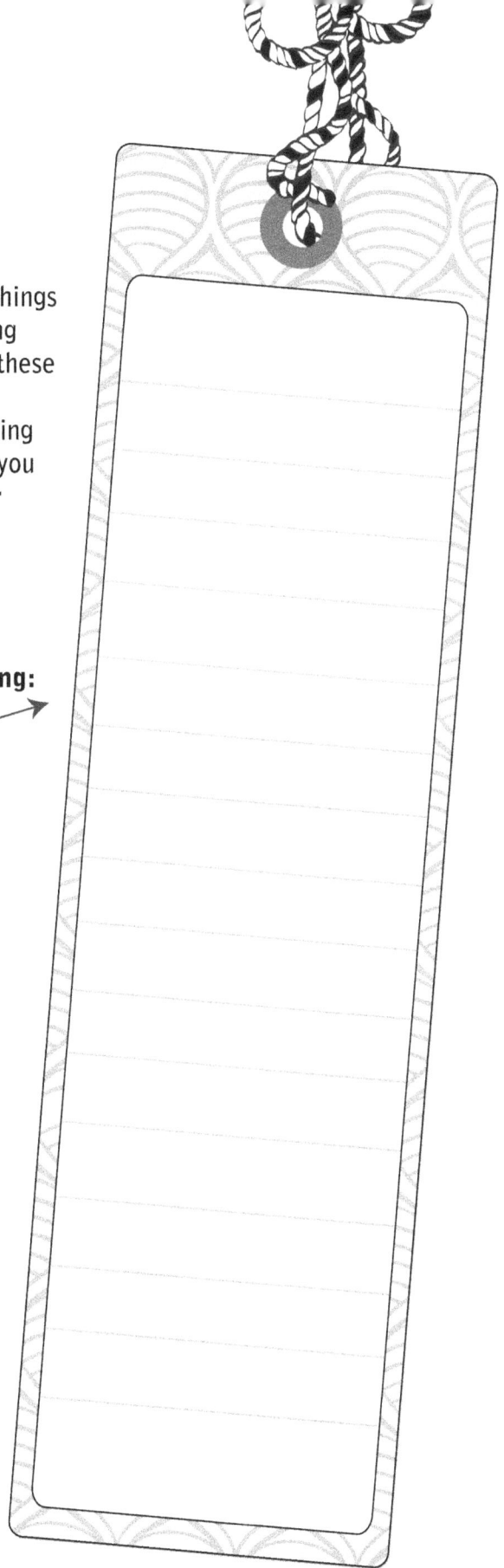

DRAW

Draw someone caring for a friend

Activity 1: Caring acts

Discuss how we care for others in many different ways.
Share some of the ways you care for others (doing something
nice for someone, being kind, being helpful...)
Look at the children on page 45 and together come up with what
you think they are doing or may have done to show that they care for others.
Colour the pictures.

NEED:
Activity page 45 []
Colouring tools []

Activity 2: Caring for a little seed

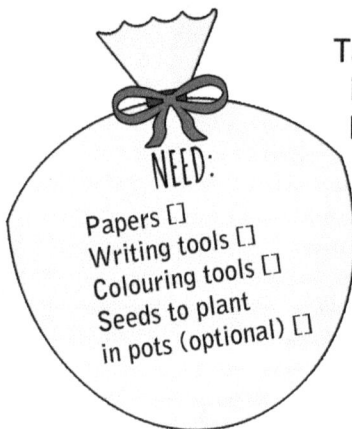

NEED:
Papers []
Writing tools []
Colouring tools []
Seeds to plant
in pots (optional) []

Talk about how a little seed needs care and love to help it grow
into something great. Explain how a seed has the potential to
become a small flower or a great big tree.

Have the children draw a little seed in the center of the paper
and around it draw different things the seed could become.
Draw what you can do to care for the little seed and make
sure it grows. If possible, plant a seed and care for it.

Ways to bring up Caring:

♥ Notice when the children act in a caring manner and encourage
these actions with verbal encouragement (example: I see that you
are showing a lot of care towards your little brother... What a great
example of caring!)

♥ When you notice someone being caring, point it out.

♥ Allow the children to help with more delicate activities that need
special amounts of care. Make sure to explain what is needed of them.
Encourage and guide them along the way.

♥ Find books that talk about caring and make sure you guide the conversation
to go beyond the book.

♥ Come up with a special project you can do together
to show how much you care for someone else.

2. Cleanliness

One way to explain Cleanliness:

We practice cleanliness by keeping our bodies, thoughts and things as clean as possible.
When we keep our rooms neat and make an effort to keep our things organized,
we are practicing cleanliness. Cleanliness can mean keeping our selves clean or making sure
we don't put anything dangerous in our mouths.
We can keep our hearts clean by not saying bad words
or hurtful things to others.

A beautiful quote about Cleanliness:

Write down a quote that you wish
to memorize or remember.
If you cannot find a quote to inspire you,
try coming up with your own.

Colouring page: See page 63

Talk about the drawing:

What are Neema
and Bella doing to
keep their room clean?

How do you
keep your
body clean?

What can you do
to help keep
your room clean?

DRAW

Draw someone
practicing cleanliness

Activity 1: Broken plate puzzle

NEED:
Activity page 47 []
Paper []
Scissors []
Glue []
Colouring tools []

Look at the plate on page 47 and help cut the pieces
to turn the plate into many pieces of a puzzle. Explain that this
is a broken plate and you need help putting it back together.
Once you have completed the puzzle, glue it back together on a
different paper and colour the final image. Discuss why it is important
to practice cleanliness and what would happen if you left a broken plate on the floor.

Activity 2: What do you use this for?

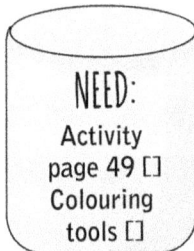

NEED:
Activity page 49 []
Colouring tools []

Discuss the importance of personal cleanliness.
Look at the items on page 49 and find the necessary
items for the following actions:
Taking a bath, blowing your nose, cutting your fingernails,
brushing your teeth, and cleaning up a spill in the kitchen.

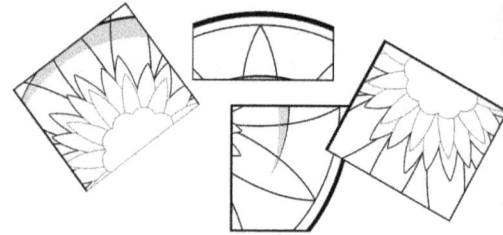

Go through the movements and pretend to actually perform the cleaning action.
Colour the things on the page and see if you can think of other things you clean regularly.

Ways to bring up Cleanliness:

♥ After playing with a toy and before moving on to another activity,
remind the children of the importance of cleaning up.

♥ Arrange the materials you use so that they are easy to put back and keep organized.
Involve them in the process. Think easy access, organization by categories, and labelling
to make sure everything has a specific place.

♥ Discuss the reasons for shower or bath time and what would be the consequences
if we did not practice cleanliness.

♥ Make a game of it. Take some old socks and create a dusting game.
When outdoors, have the children help with messy activities and cleaning up.

♥ Choose some cleaning music.

3. Cooperation

One way to explain Cooperation:

Cooperation means working together with other people. Good cooperation takes place when everyone feels happy about their contribution and when everyone has made an effort to work together. When cooperating with others it is important to be patient and kind and make sure everyone gets a chance to participate.

A beautiful quote about Cooperation:

Write down a quote that you wish to memorize or remember. If you cannot find a quote to inspire you, try coming up with your own.

Colouring page: See page 65

Talk about the drawing:

How do you think Tom and Zara cooperate when they play together?

Can you think of ways you cooperate well with others?

DRAW

Draw children cooperating on a project

Activity 1: Abstract art mosaic

Cut a paper in small squares. Distribute 6 pieces per child and have them draw and colour each of the pieces. Discuss how beautiful art can be created from all these little pieces put together the same way amazing things can happen when people cooperate. Once all the pieces have a pattern or design of their own, have the children work together to create a new image using all the little pieces. Glue on a new sheet of paper and admire. Discuss how everyone cooperated to make the new piece.

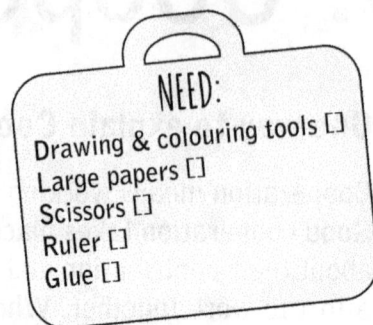

NEED:
Drawing & colouring tools []
Large papers []
Scissors []
Ruler []
Glue []

Activity 2: Cooperative art

Using a ruler, divide a large sheet of paper into smaller sections. The sections do not need to be of equal size or shape. Explain that every 20 seconds you will call "switch" and at that time everyone will begin to work on a different part of the paper. Have each child pick a section of the paper and draw or decorate it as they wish. Explain how each child can either finish someone's drawing or start a new one in a different space. Every 20 seconds, call "switch" and switch places so all the children have the opportunity to work on all sections of the paper. If there are only two of you, take turns. Let the children organize themselves around the paper and intervene only if necessary. Keep calling "switch" until all the spaces on the paper are filled. Admire the final image together and discuss how it felt to complete each other's work.

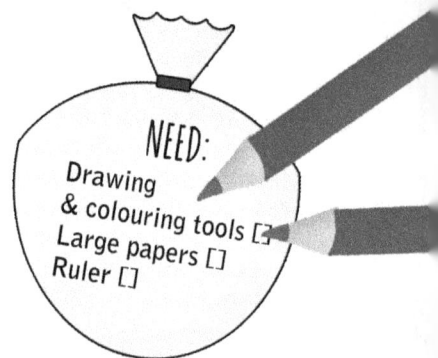

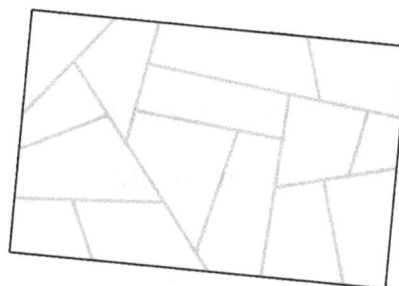

NEED:
Drawing & colouring tools []
Large papers []
Ruler []

Ways to bring up Cooperation:

💜 Acknowledge all efforts made to work with others.

💜 Use terms such as participation, collaboration and sharing more often.

💜 During teamwork, emphasize how individual success is not as important as the success of the team that works together to accomplish a desired task.

4. Compassion

One way to explain Compassion:

Compassion means trying to imagine, understand, and have empathy for what others may be going through. When we care about people, we can show compassion by being loving and patient with them. We can show compassion by forgiving others for making mistakes and by being kind to people who are feeling hurt or sad.

A beautiful quote about Compassion:

Write down a quote that you wish to memorize or remember. If you cannot find a quote to inspire you, try coming up with your own.

Colouring page: See page 67

Talk about the drawing:

Can you think of another way Jake could help Maya now that she has hurt her knee?

How do you show someone compassion?

Imagine that Maya is your friend. How would you feel if she was hurt?

Design a compassion badge

Activity 1: Potato people

Preparation: Prepare the potatoes by transforming them into potato stamps. Cut off a small piece from the top to flatten the stamping part, then cut around the potato to make the shape of the stamp leaving the remainder as the base for holding. You need two shapes for this activity: squares and triangles.

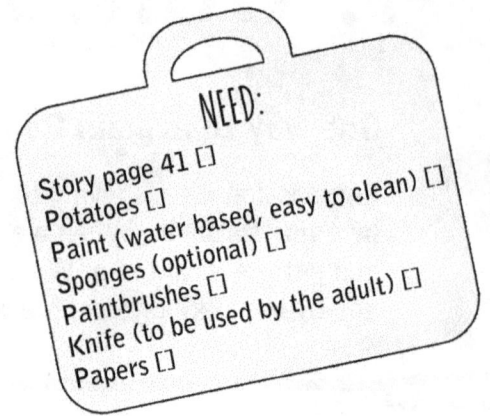

NEED:
Story page 41 []
Potatoes []
Paint (water based, easy to clean) []
Sponges (optional) []
Paintbrushes []
Knife (to be used by the adult) []
Papers []

Potato people: Read the story on page 41 and have the children illustrate the story using the potato stamps and paint. Determine when is the right time to pause and make a drawing (see suggestions in the story). Make sure the drawings are simple and quick so the children don't lose momentum or interest. If you feel that too much attention is given to the drawings, read the story all at once before stamping.

Activity 2: Mobile Phones

NEED:
Cardboard []
Scissors []
Colouring tools []
Papers []

Discuss how compassion can sometimes be like consideration, meaning that we must think carefully about some of the things we do because they can make others feel angry or sad. Cut a rectangular piece of cardboard and have each child decorate their cardboard to make it look like a mobile phone. Have everyone draw the numbers and decorate it. Create different ring tones for each phone. Come up with different scenarios and together decide where and when it would be appropriate to use a phone and when it would be inconsiderate and might bother other people. Discuss other ways we can be considerate, like giving our seat to others on the bus or helping people carry their groceries.

Make a drawing of someone being compassionate towards someone else.

Ways to bring up Compassion:

When you see other people in public looking sad or acting in certain ways, discuss what could possibly be happening in their lives and how we can show compassion.

Offer encouragement to any deeds of kindness and compassion shown, especially towards friends, other siblings or family members.

Make cards or bake cookies for someone who is sick or not feeling well. Have everyone participate in the activity.

Role play.

5. Courage

One way to explain Courage:

We show courage when we do something that is hard for us. We show courage when we do something even though we may be afraid to do it, or think that we are not capable. Some people must be courageous everyday by doing things that are dangerous and by being very brave.

A beautiful quote about Courage:
Write down a quote that you wish to memorize or remember. If you cannot find a quote to inspire you, try coming up with your own.

Colouring page: See page 69

Talk about the drawing:

Can you think of something that you do that shows courage?

How is Basanti being courageous?

Do you know any courageous people?

DRAW

Draw a courageous animal and create a story to go with your drawing

Activity 1: Courageous people

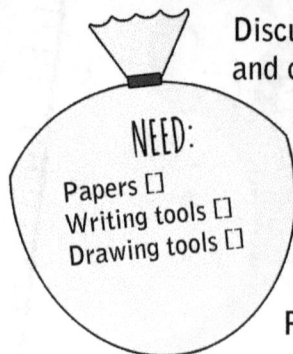

NEED:
Papers []
Writing tools []
Drawing tools []

Discuss different types of jobs in which people may need to show extra courage and come up with questions you would ask them if you could meet them.

If you know any of these people in your community go and ask them your questions at a later time. In the meantime come up with what you think they may answer. Can you think of some of the things these people might do when they are afraid that helps them show courage? Make a nice drawing of the courageous people doing these jobs.

Possible questions:

What do you do when you are afraid?
What's the best part of your job?
How do you describe courage?

Activity 2: Courageous animals

Talk about different animals. Create stories about these animals and have them show courage in the stories. Look at pictures of the animals for inspiration and have the children draw or paint the faces of these brave animals on masks. Help by making holes for the string as well as for the eyes. Have everyone wear their masks and pretend to be a brave animal.

Create a play and act out your stories.

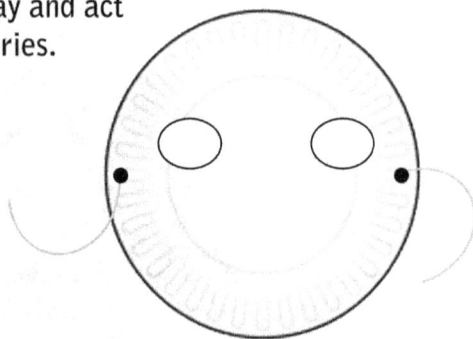

NEED:

Paper plates []
String []
Hole punch (you can also use scissors) []
Paint or colouring tools []
Scissors (adult help required) []
Optional: pictures of different animals []

Ways to bring up Courage:

♥ Acknowledge efforts made to overcome fear or personal challenges.

♥ Read stories of heroic individuals (vary and combine stories of fictional characters and stories of actual people).

♥ When watching television or movies, talk about what you see. When appropriate, explain what is happening and include words such as courage, bravery, perseverance and patience.

6. Creativity

One way to explain Creativity:

Creativity is a way of doing things using our imagination.
Sometimes it means looking at things in a different way,
or finding unusual ways of solving problems.
Being creative means using your talents, your imagination
or your unique qualities to create things that can be
unusual, fun or different. You should never be afraid
to be creative and unique in what you do or who you are.

A beautiful quote about Creativity:

Write down a quote that you wish
to memorize or remember.
If you cannot find a quote to inspire you,
try coming up with your own.

Colouring page: See page 71

Talk about the drawing:

In which way are
Katinka and Tiko
showing their creativity?

How are you
creative?

DRAW

Draw children
being creative

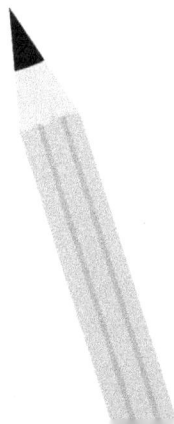

Activity 1: Junk art

*If possible, find different images showing recycled art from around the world. Share these to show how creativity can take on many forms.

Discuss how being creative means seeing things differently and in unusual ways. Place all the items on a table and together or individually create different art pieces using the items found. Give a title to each piece and make a small exhibit. Discuss how it felt to make art from all these items.

NEED:
Things from your recycling box []
Any materials from around the house []
Scissors []
Tape or glue []
Colouring tools []
Writing tools []
Other decorative items []

Activity 2: Use your imagination

NEED:
Colouring tools []
Papers []

Explain how this game consists of using our imagination to create a picture inside our mind. Sit together and imagine that you are tiny creatures. What do you look like as a tiny creature? Describe the creatures together. Then imagine you are a giant or a cat. What kind of cat would you be? Imagine you are a flower. What do you smell like? Make sure everyone takes a turn and give a bit of time for each child to create a picture in his or her mind.

Draw a picture of what you saw in your mind.

Ways to bring up Creativity:

💜 Be creative. The children will enjoy doing things with you and feel encouraged to develop their own creativity.

💜 Have the children play with all kinds of toys, especially games and toys that they create.

💜 Encourage looking at things in different ways.

💜 Encourage finding different solutions to different problems.

💜 Have fun, be messy, create new games, or invent new recipes.

7. Determination

One way to explain Determination:

Determination is when we make an effort to finish something that is hard for us. When something takes a long time to learn, when we need a lot of courage and persistence to finish something hard and still manage to complete it, then we show determination. We can show determination when we learn a new sport, finish difficult homework or when we don't give up on something we want to accomplish.

Colouring page: See page 73

Talk about the drawing:

How does Pierre shows determination in learning a new sport?

What have you done lately that took a lot of determination?

A beautiful quote about Determination:

Write down a quote that you wish to memorize or remember.
If you cannot find a quote to inspire you, try coming up with your own.

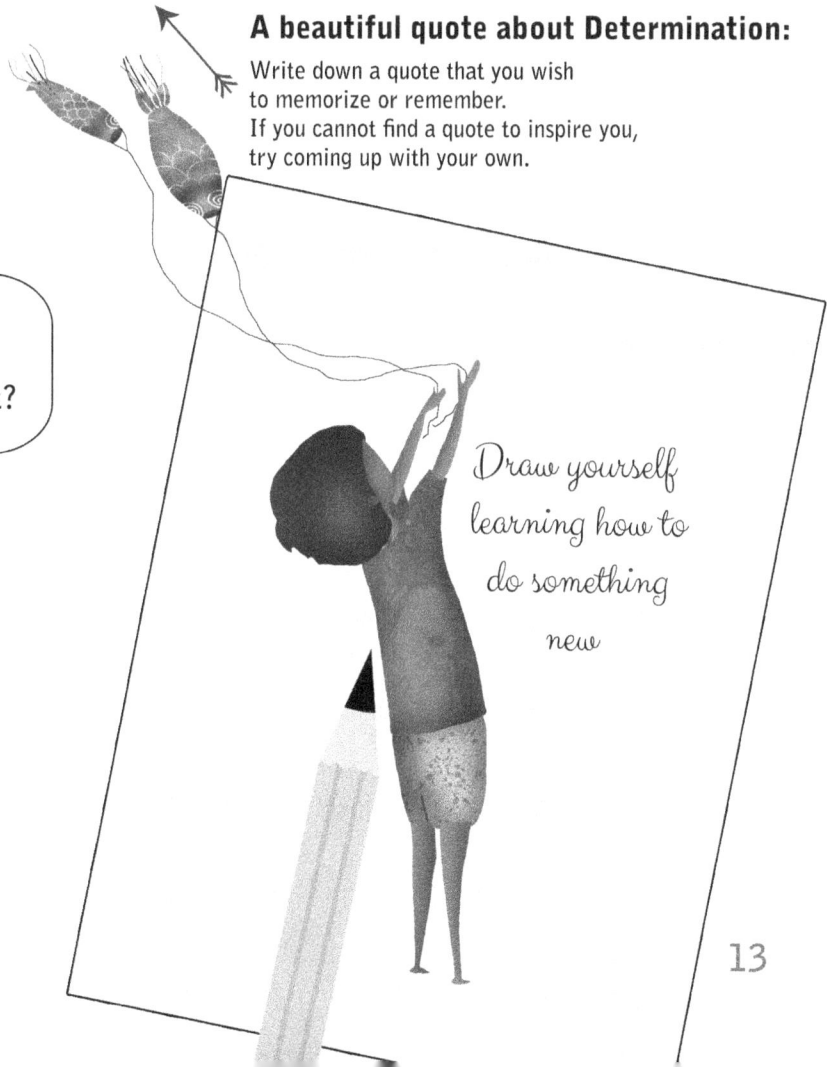

Draw yourself learning how to do something new

Activity 1: Follow the shadow

Decide together who should be the first leader. Dim the lights of the room and place the lamp in such a way as to create a shadow on the wall. Have the first leader move around and create different shadows while the rest follow behind and try to recreate the same shadows. Decide together who should be the second leader and so on and make sure everyone gets a turn as leader. Discuss how hard it is sometimes to do something that takes a lot of effort and how determination can help us succeed.

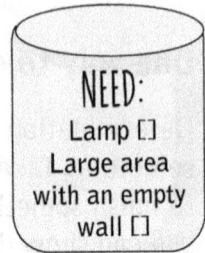

NEED:
Lamp []
Large area with an empty wall []

Activity 2: Listen, Freeze, Go

Discuss how determination takes a lot of patience because you have to go through many challenges before you succeed. Come up with a list of different instructions such as "stand on one foot" or "jump around" and call them out loud. Then say "freeze".

Skip around the chair!

Run to the corner!

Jump towards the table!

The children have to remain frozen in their position until you say "go". You may have to do a couple of trial runs.

Vary the requests as well as the amount of time to wait.

Take turns calling out the instruction.

Ways to bring up Determination:

♥ When reading a book or watching television, point out the efforts made by the hero or heroine and discuss how they showed determination.

♥ When something is accomplished that showed a great amount of determination, reward the action by doing something nice or giving appropriate praise (not everything deserves a gift, yet some efforts are worth making a big deal about).

♥ Encourage children to finish what they start. Lead by example.

8. Forgiveness

One way to explain Forgiveness:

Forgiveness is a virtue that helps us have understanding, patience and love for those around us. When we forgive someone, we no longer feel angry at them or feel upset. We are able to listen to what they have to say and accept their apologies. Forgiveness allows us to bring love back into our hearts when we are angry.
If we make a mistake, we should apologize sincerely and ask the other person to forgive us.

A beautiful quote about Forgiveness:

Write down a quote that you wish to memorize or remember.
If you cannot find a quote to inspire you, try coming up with your own.

Colouring page: See page 75

Talk about the drawing:

Do you think it's easy for Tom to forgive Kiara for breaking his castle?

Have you ever forgiven someone for breaking something of yours?

What do you think Kiara said to Tom when she found out where her ball went?

DRAW

Draw someone practicing forgiveness

Activity 1: The story of the stubborn pig

Read the story on page 42 and have everyone decide together on the ending. Will the other animals forgive the stubborn pig? Draw the ending that you have created.

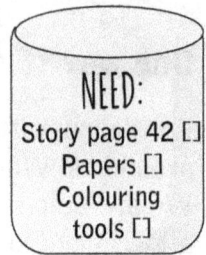

NEED:
Story page 42 []
Papers []
Colouring tools []

Activity 2: Happy or sad

Using the circular shape create two faces on the paper. Make one a happy face and the other a sad face. Help by cutting the faces out if necessary. Read the following scenarios. After reading each scenario take a short pause while everyone raises the face they think best shows how the person you are reading about feels. Discuss your answers together.

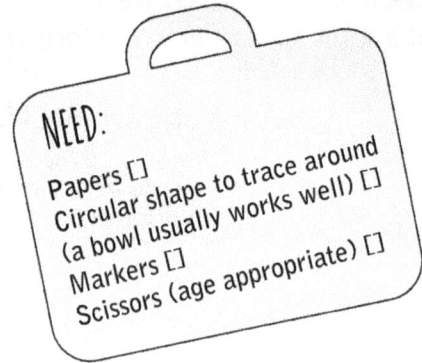

NEED:
Papers []
Circular shape to trace around (a bowl usually works well) []
Markers []
Scissors (age appropriate) []

1. Tony broke his mother's flower pot. How does Tony feel?

2. Tony's mother just came home to find the flower pot. How does she feel?

3. Tony explains that it was an accident and that he is very sorry. How does Tony feel after saying that?

4. Tony's mother forgives him for breaking the flower pot.
She is proud of him for telling the truth. How does she feel?

5. Marie is very angry at her baby brother for making a mess in her room. How does she feel?

6. Marie's mother explains that her baby brother is still very young and that he didn't mean to make a mess. Marie decides to forgive her baby brother. How does she feel now?

7. Norah apologized for throwing all the toys on the floor, but Tom is still angry and doesn't want to forgive her. How does Norah feel? How does Tom feel?

8. Ayan decided to forgive his friend for accidently bumping into him.
They are now playing together again. How do you think they feel?

Ways to bring up Forgiveness:

💜 Take the habit of saying "I'm sorry" for all mistakes.

💜 Explain that showing forgiveness is something that helps everyone.
Show love to others even when they make mistakes.

💜 Create a routine associated with saying sorry, forgiving, hugging and moving on.

9. Generosity

One way to explain Generosity:

Generosity comes from the love we have in our hearts. Generosity makes us want to share what we have with the people we love as well as with those who have less than us. We can learn to be generous by sharing what we have, giving things away when others don't have much, or opening our hearts and our homes.

A beautiful quote about Generosity:
Write down a quote that you wish to memorize or remember. If you cannot find a quote to inspire you, try coming up with your own.

Colouring page: See page 77

Talk about the drawing:

How do you think Sheila felt when she realized she had nothing in her lunch box?

How do you think Sheila and Mei Lee feel after sharing some food together?

DRAW

Make a nice drawing of yourself being generous

17

Activity 1: Share the pie

*You can also have actual food and have the children divide it among everyone present. You may want to do this after the activity.

Draw a large circle and pretend that it is a pie. Have the children colour the pie with their favourite colours. Suggest toppings that they can draw on the pie to make it extra delicious. Discuss together with whom they would like to share the pie and help them cut out the right number of pieces so that the pie can be shared with all the people they suggested. Follow up this activity with actual food sharing.

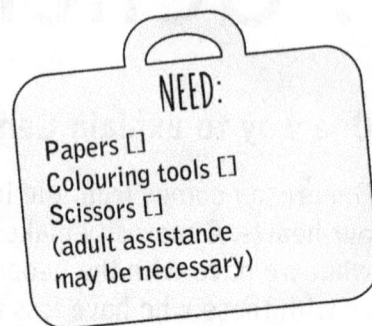

NEED:
Papers []
Colouring tools []
Scissors []
(adult assistance may be necessary)

Activity 2: Generous ants

Discuss the qualities of ants. Did you know that even thought ants are very small insects, they can carry up to ten times their size? When an ant finds a good pile of food, instead of keeping it for itself, it will leave a trail so that all the other ants can find it as well. Isn't that generous? Look at the maze on page 51 and see if you can help the little ant find where the food is and leave a trail for the others. Make a nice drawing of an ant sharing some food with others and place your drawing somewhere where you can look at it and remember how generous ants are. If you can, go outside and look at some real ants.

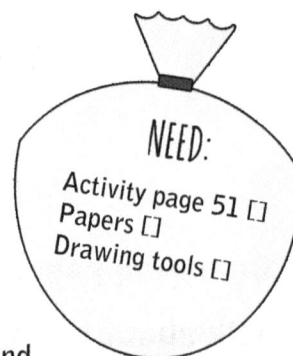

NEED:
Activity page 51 []
Papers []
Drawing tools []

Ways to bring up Generosity:

💜Be generous in whatever ways you can. Encourage and invite children to participate and get involved in your efforts.

💜Volunteer and help out when you can. It doesn't have to be a big project to make a difference. Something as simple as doing something nice for a neighbour can make a big difference. Get the children to help out or create their own projects.

💜Donate to different organizations. Go through clothes, toys, and other accumulated things. Organize a donation drive in your neighborhood.

💜Invite people into your home.

10. Gentleness

One way to explain Gentleness:

Gentleness is how we do things in a soft, caring, and careful manner. We always need to do our best to be gentle and kind with everyone. We can use a gentle voice or be gentle in how we do things. We can also be gentle by thinking of others and doing nice things for them.

A beautiful quote about Gentleness:

Write down a quote that you wish to memorize or remember.
If you cannot find a quote to inspire you, try coming up with your own.

Colouring page: See page 79

Talk about the drawing:

Why do you think Isaac is being gentle with his new kitten?

How does Isaac practice gentleness?

How are you gentle with others?

DRAW

Draw someone being gentle

Activity 1: Big hands little hands

Have the children trace their hand.
Next to that have them draw out a much bigger hand (they can trace
yours). Have them colour the different hands. Discuss the difference
between things that we do with our little hands that require gentleness, tenderness and
being very careful and things that we get to do with our big hands which require less attention.
Cut out the different hands and make sure that everyone has at least one big and one little hand.
Explain how you will give different examples of things that we do either with big hands or little
hands. When you suggest something that should be done with little hands, have everyone very
quietly raise the little hand. When you suggest something that can be done with big hands,
have the children make a lot of noise and raise the big hand.

Here are some examples of different situations you can suggest.
Make sure to add your own and welcome suggestions from everyone involved.

Playing with a baby.	Gardening outside.
Catching the ball outside.	Putting someone to sleep.
Holding an egg.	Playing in the park.

Activity 2: Pouring game

*Potentially messy game, ideal as an outdoor activity

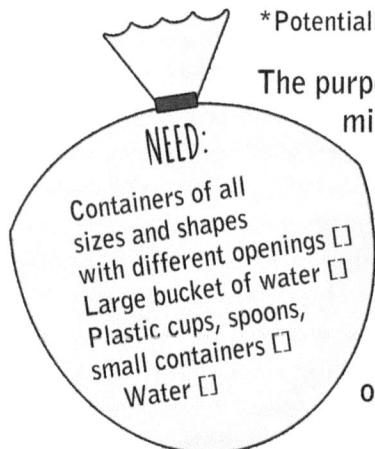

The purpose of this game is to fill up as many containers as possible with a
minimum amount of water spilled. Explain that to avoid spilling
the children have to be gentle, patient, and work together. Choose
containers with very little openings as well as some with large ones.
Line up all the containers on a waterproof cloth (or outdoors).
Have the children fill their small containers or spoons from the large
bucket of water and fill all the containers with water. Make sure
everyone gets a turn. Have fun with this activity and discuss
other activities that require us to be gentle.

Ways to bring up Gentleness:

💚 Talk about using gentle voices and gentle hands.

💚 Play games that require gentleness and coordination.

💚 Balance the time for the children to be quiet and gentle with time
when they can make a lot of noise. Sing songs that allow for quiet and loud voices.

11. Helpfulness

One way explain Helpfulness:

We are helpful when we do things to help others, like when we offer assistance to make things easier for them. You don't have to be strong or very old to be helpful. Everyone can be helpful by doing small things to help or by having a helpful attitude.

A beautiful quote about Helpfulness:

Write down a quote that you wish to memorize or remember.
If you cannot find a quote to inspire you, try coming up with your own.

Colouring page: See page 81

Talk about the drawing:

How is Itach being helpful?

How do you think Itach's mother feels knowing she has such a helpful son?

What can you do to be helpful?

Draw yourself being helpful

Activity 1: Help with Cookies

*Feel free to use your own cookie recipe.

Discuss your plan to make cookies together and what would be helpful in preparing the cookies. Read the recipe together and discuss what steps you can do to create as little of a mess as possible. Decide in advance how you are each going to help with cleaning and only then follow the recipe together. As you prepare the cookies, ask questions regarding the importance of helping others. Once you have baked your cookies, make sure you all follow through with your cleaning responsibilities. Prepare some cookies to give out as a surprise.

Preheat oven to 375° F and line cookie sheets with wax paper. If you don't have any wax (or parchment) paper, oil your cookie sheet.

Combine flour, cinnamon, baking soda, salt, your choice of nuts, quick oats and raisins in a medium sized bowl.

Beat the eggs and the vegetable oil in a different bowl. Mix in the teaspoon of vanilla extract.

Mix everything together.

Flour (1 Cup)   Cinnamon (1 teaspoon)
Baking soda (1 teaspoon)   Salt (1/2 teaspoon)
Your favourite nuts (1/2 Cup)   2 Eggs
Quick oats – not instant (1 Cup)
Raisins or dried cranberries (1 Cup)
Applesauce (1 Cup)
Vegetable Oil (1/2 Cup)
Vanilla Extract (1 teaspoon)

Using a tablespoon, drop the cookie dough onto the baking sheet making sure to leave about an inch between each cookie.

Bake for about 8 to 10 minutes   Let cool, enjoy and share. Don't forget to clean up!

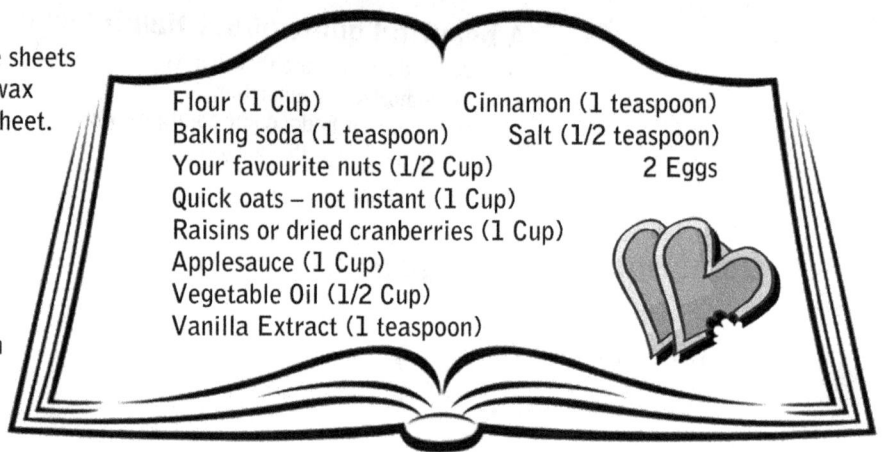

Activity 2: Kika the little bird

Read the story. Discuss different ways of being helpful and whether or not you can ever be too small to help others.

NEED:
Story page 43 []
Colouring tools []
Papers []

Help fold a paper in half to make a card. On the front have everyone make a drawing of Kika being very helpful. Give the card and share the story with someone you love.

Ways to bring up Helpfulness:

♥ Help children be responsible for simple things and thank them for doing them (setting the table, getting the mail, recycling, or whatever you feel he or she is able to do).

♥ Give specific tasks that make it easier for children to know how to be helpful at times.

♥Allow and encourage helpful behaviour in all areas of your lives.

12. Honesty

One way to explain Honesty:

Honesty means telling the truth and doing what we believe is right. We are honest when we try our best to keep our promises, tell the truth, and make an effort to be fair and just. Being honest means trying to be the best we can be.

A beautiful quote about Honesty:

Write down a quote that you wish to memorize or remember.
If you cannot find a quote to inspire you, try coming up with your own.

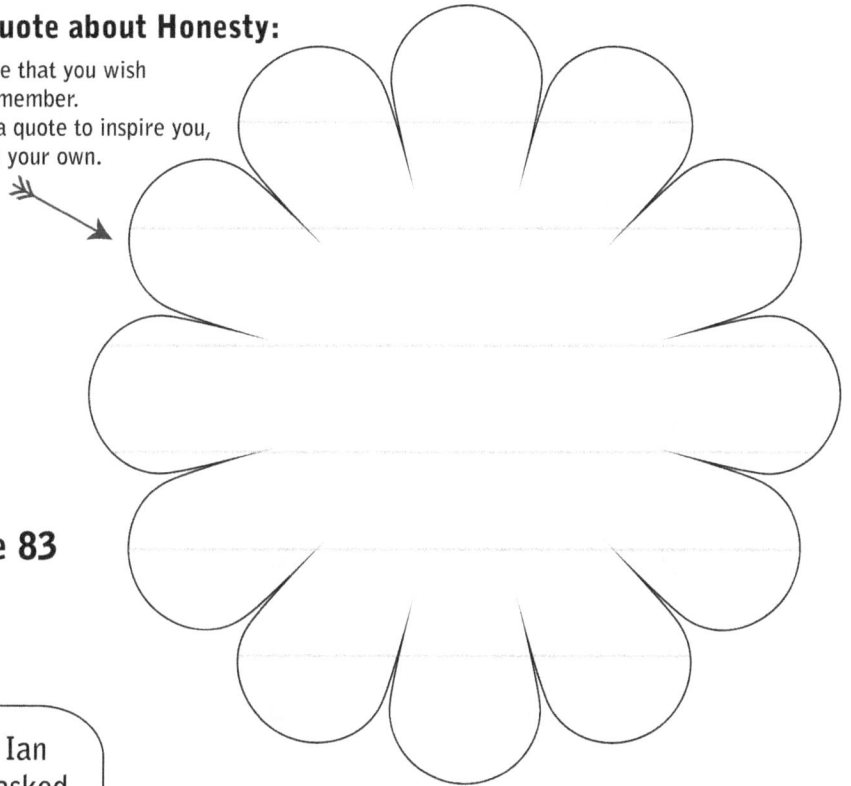

Colouring page: See page 83

Talk about the drawing:

Can you guess how Ian felt when his father asked him where the sheep was?

Do you think Ian's father is proud of Ian for telling the truth?

Do you think Ian was afraid that his father would be upset?

Have you ever told the truth even when it was very hard?

Draw yourself being honest in a difficult situation

Activity 1: Me and Not me

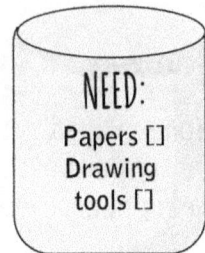

NEED:
Papers []
Drawing
tools []

Have everyone draw two characters. Call one of them **Me** and the other
Not me. Explain how **Me** tells the truth and is always honest, while
Not me tries to get out of every situation, lies, and often comes up
with crazy answers so he/she won't have to apologize or fix his/her mistakes.

Come up with different scenarios and discuss how each character would respond.

Examples of scenarios:

They have just broken a vase in the kitchen but there was no one around to see who did it.
What will they tell their mother?

They have forgotten their lunch bag at school and their father is looking everywhere for it.

Come up with other examples together and continue discussing
which is the better way to behave and why.

Activity 2: Tiny the little brown pony

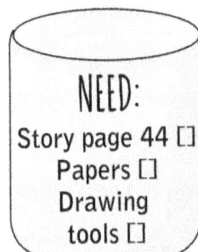

NEED:
Story page 44 []
Papers []
Drawing
tools []

Read the story on page 44 together and come up with 2 different endings,
one showing honesty and one in which Tiny is not being honest.

Draw pictures of your two different endings or pick the one you like best
or draw a picture of that ending only.

Ways to bring up Honesty:

💜 Avoid labelling and seeing things in black and white. Teach children that we all make
mistakes and that even if we have done something wrong, we still need to tell the truth.

💜 Praise honesty and uncover the reasons for telling a lie. Discuss cheating while playing
games and encourage honesty. Explain why lying doesn't make any situation better.

💜 Explain the meaning of "white lies". Talk about saying positive things and trying to
find good things to say.

💜 Explore different games that deal with telling the truth and lying.

13. Joyfulness

One way to explain Joyfulness:

Being joyful means being happy and wanting to share that feeling of happiness with others. When we are joyful we are full of love and we want to do things to make others happy. We want to have fun and share laughter with others.

A beautiful quote about Joyfulness:

Write down a quote that you wish to memorize or remember. If you cannot find a quote to inspire you, try coming up with your own.

Colouring page: See page 85

Talk about the drawing:

Do you have special people in your life that make you feel joyful?

Do Maria and Aisha seem joyful to you?

What do you see on their faces that makes you think they are happy?

DRAW

Draw yourself feeling joyful

Activity 1: Drawing joyful faces

Talk about what a joyful face looks like. Describe it together
and use the mirror to make different faces. Make angry faces,
sad faces, happy and joyful faces. Look at the children on page 53
and notice how they have been drawn without faces. Draw faces
on them that show joyfulness. Colour the picture of the joyful children.

Come up with a story together about why you think the children are joyful.

NEED:
Activity page 53 []
Mirror []
Colouring tools []

Activity 2: Joyful bowling

NEED:
Lots of
toilet paper rolls []
Different objects
from around the house []
Masking tape []

The purpose of this activity is to help children have fun in a creative way.
Use the toilet paper rolls as pins (or any other unbreakable items from your
recycling box). Set them down in a triangular formation and associate a
certain number of points with each pin (colour code them if you wish).
Let children pick their own bowling objects to bowl with. Have them
choose 2-3 objects each (shoes, toy cars, plastic containers...).
Use the tape to mark the lanes. Make sure to remove all breakables.

Have fun! This is also a great party game!

Ways to bring up Joyfulness:

💜 Have fun. Laughter and joy are contagious.

💜 Do at least one thing a week with the sole purpose of bringing joy into your life.

💜 Share your favourite childhood experiences.

💜 Watch funny movies.

💜 Have a party for no reason. Make everyone wear funny hats!

💜 Sing and dance.

💜 Have a water fight or a snow fight. Whatever the season.

💜 Play.

14. Justice

One way to explain Justice:

Being just means doing what we feel is right
by listening to what our heart is telling us.
Justice means being fair with ourselves and others
and looking for the truth. Being just means
understanding that if we do something that
we shouldn't do, we will have to apologize
or make up for our actions.

A beautiful quote about Justice:

Write down a quote that you wish
to memorize or remember.
If you cannot find a quote to inspire you,
try coming up with your own.

Colouring page: See page 87

Talk about the drawing:

How does Wanni show
that she can be fair in sharing
the pie with her friend?

How would Wanni's friend feel
if she got a very small piece
while Wanni took a very big
piece of pie for herself?

How can
you be just
with others?

DRAW

Draw
yourself
practicing
justice

Activity 1: Standing up for justice

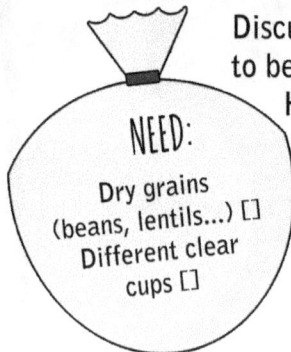

NEED:

Dry grains (beans, lentils...) []
Different clear cups []

Discuss what justice means in terms of fairness. Explain how you are trying to be fair and practice justice by dividing the grains equally between the glasses. Have everyone sit down and watch as you slowly spread the grains around. Explain that they should only stand up when they believe all the glasses have the same amount. Take your time in sharing the grains around, stopping to ask "are they all the same now?" Let the children come to their own conclusion and guide you as to which glass needs more or less. Discuss together different ways to practice justice.

Activity 2: Sharing Food

NEED:

Colouring tools []
Papers []
Scissors (age appropriate) []

Pretend that you are having a party and draw different kinds of food that you would make for your guests. You can draw cake, pizza, pie, or anything else you can think of. Decide on the number of people you wish to invite to your party and divide the food equally so that everyone gets a fair share.

Possible follow up discussions:

One person is allergic to half the food. What do you do?

One person drops everything before they have eaten their food. What happens now?

You can also have a little snack after the activity and practice dividing it equally.

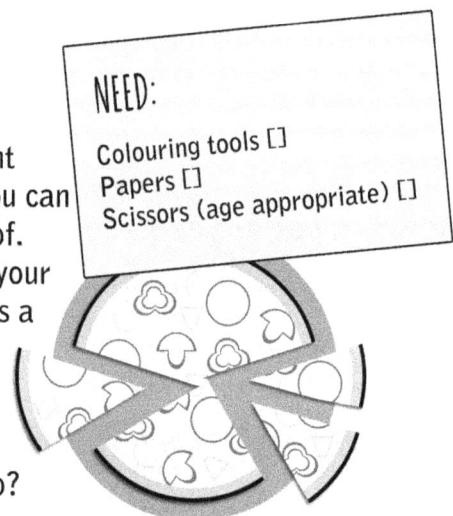

Ways to bring up Justice:

💜 Have the children be responsible for distributing and sharing certain things.

💜 Teach consequences and uphold them. Make sure children understand that the choices they make can affect other people to.

💜 When appropriate, ask them if things are fair or how others feel based on their actions.

💜 Play games in which you get a chance to talk about cheating and playing fair.

15. Kindness

One way to explain Kindness:

Kindness means caring and doing nice deeds for others. We are kind when we take care of animals and other people as well as do our best to make others happy through our actions. You can show kindness in many different ways. Saying something nice or doing something to help someone are nice ways to show kindness.

A beautiful quote about Kindness:

Write down a quote that you wish to memorize or remember.
If you cannot find a quote to inspire you, try coming up with your own.

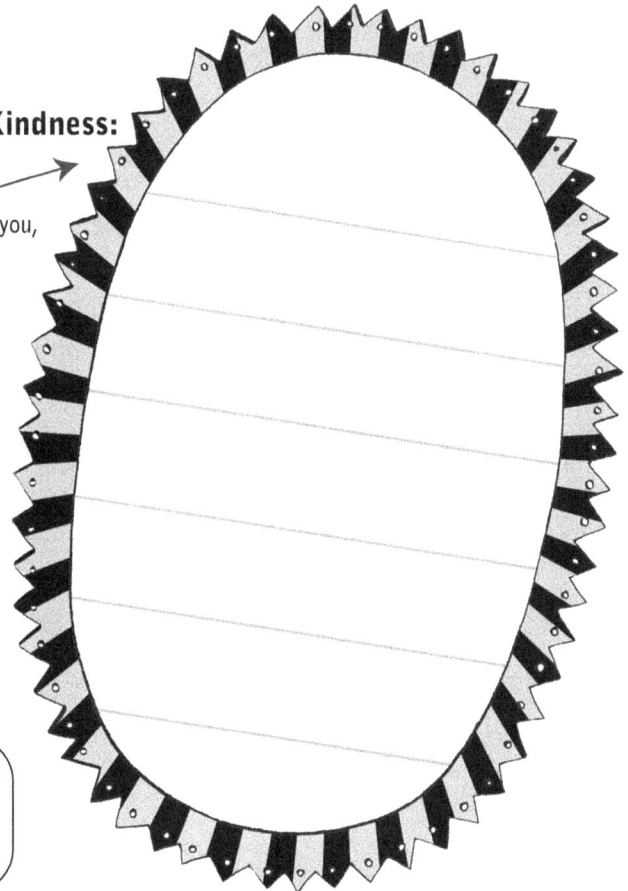

Colouring page: See page 89

Talk about the drawing:

Why do you think Aiko is helping the bird?

Can you think of something else Aiko could do to help the bird?

What can you do to show kindness?

DRAW

Draw yourself being kind to a bird

Activity 1: Fishing for kindness

Cut out all the fish cards from pages 55 and 57. With the writing hidden, place the fish cards on a table or on the floor. Explain that you are fishing for acts of kindness and that you will only keep the fish cards that describe acts of kindness. Have everyone take a turn choosing a card. Read what is written on each card and discuss if what is written describes an act of kindness. Colour the cards that show acts of kindness.

NEED:
Activity pages 55 & 57 []
Scissors []
Colouring tools []

Activity 2: Bandage finger puppets

NEED:
Empty cereal box []
Scissors (for adult) []
Paint or markers []
Decorating (sparkles, glue, images from magazines...) []
Bandages []
Pen []

Start by making the stage. Take the empty cereal box and cut a rectangular shape out of the front on the box. This will be the opening where the puppets will appear. Turn the cereal box upside down and use the opening of the box as the place where the children will put their hands. Decorate your new theatre set.

Singing a song to calm your baby brother

Not keeping your promise

Have the children draw eyes and mouths on each bandage. Place one on the index finger of each child. Create different scenarios in which the puppets are kind to each other and in which the puppets are not so kind to each other. Ask the children to decide what was better for their puppets. Create a small play about kindness.

Ways to bring up Kindness:

💜 Talk about being kind to people and animals.

💜 Give children a chance to develop their sense of kindness by encouraging their initiative to be generous and charitable.

💜 When you need to correct improper behaviour, have the children demonstrate what would have been the proper behaviour instead.

💜 Have a "do something nice" day where everyone does something kind for someone else.

💜 Read stories about kindness.

16. Love

One way to explain Love:

Love is how we show that we care for other people. When we love someone, we want to be close to them, do nice things for them, and share with them the joy that they bring to us. We show our love by telling others that we love them or by doing nice things for them.

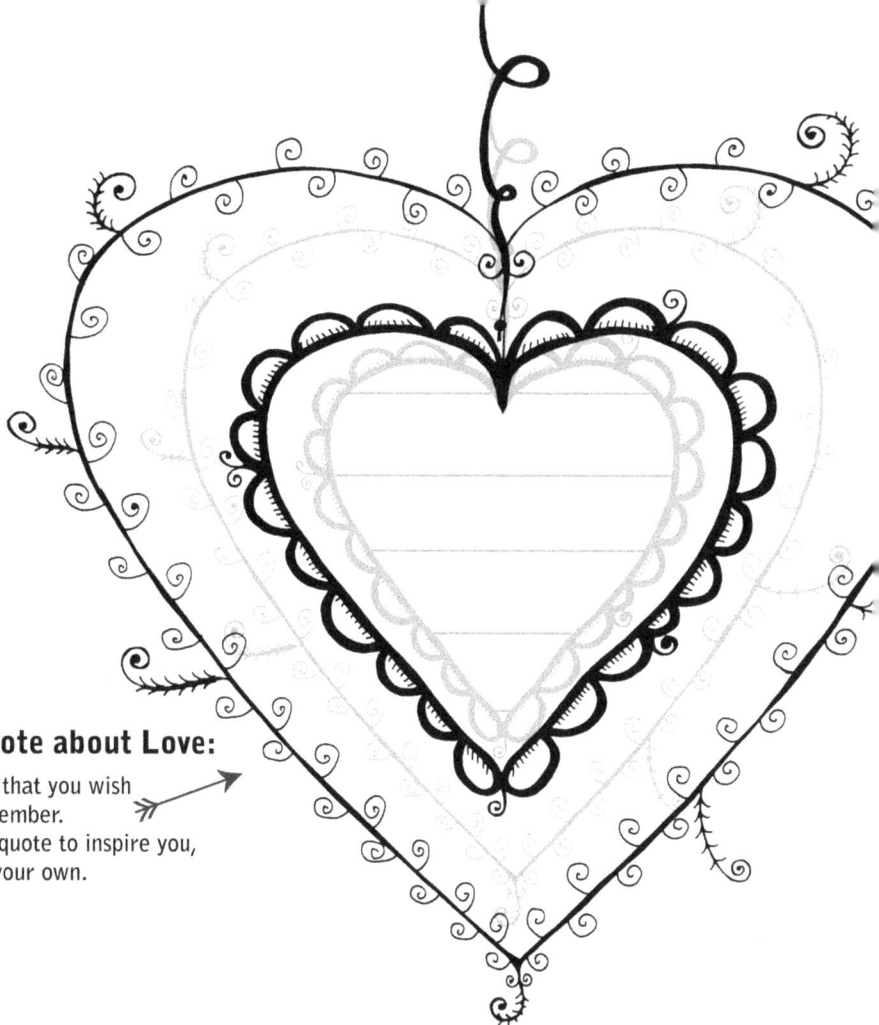

A beautiful quote about Love:

Write down a quote that you wish to memorize or remember.
If you cannot find a quote to inspire you, try coming up with your own.

Colouring page: See page 91

Talk about the drawing:

What do you usually say to someone you love?

How else can Sumie show her love?

In how many languages can you say "I love you"?

DRAW

Draw someone sharing their love

Activity 1: Show your love

Discuss how when you care for someone you do things to show them that you love them. You can do a service for someone or make them something nice. Think of a person you love and decide what you want to do for them. Think of an easy service you can do like helping in the garden, setting the table, putting away your toys without being asked or anything else you may want to do. Make them a card to show them how much you love them. Have the children decide on what service they are going to do to show their love for someone else. Fold your paper in two and make a nice drawing on the top. Give it to someone you love.

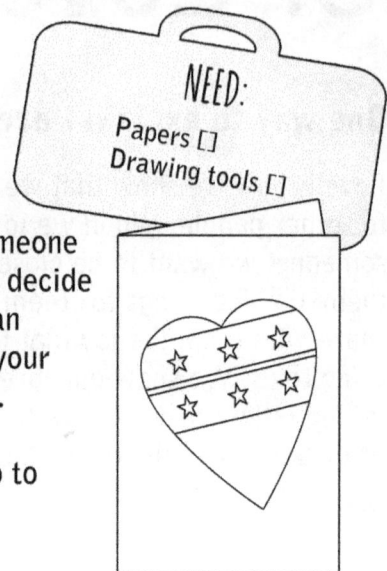

Activity 2: Caring for an imaginary pet

Discuss how when you love someone you have to do your best to take proper care of them. Talk about different animals that you have or would like to have as pets. Pick an animal that you love and draw a picture of it. Give it a name and cut it out. On a different piece of paper, draw or write (help may be needed with the writing) all the things you can do to love and care for this animal properly. Keep your little animal and care for it as your new imaginary pet.

Ways to bring up Love:

♥ Say "I love you" often.

♥ Talk about different kinds of love.

♥ Make cards to tell family and friends that you love them (grandparents especially love receiving these).

♥ Celebrate accomplishments, birthdays, and anniversaries. Make these occasions about celebrating your love for each other, not about receiving gifts.

♥ Create new family traditions.

17. Patience

One way to explain Patience:

We practice being patient when we wait for something or someone without being angry or upset, or when we don't make others feel bad for being late. We can show patience by taking the time to do something well instead of rushing through it.

A beautiful quote about Patience:

Write down a quote that you wish to memorize or remember.
If you cannot find a quote to inspire you, try coming up with your own.

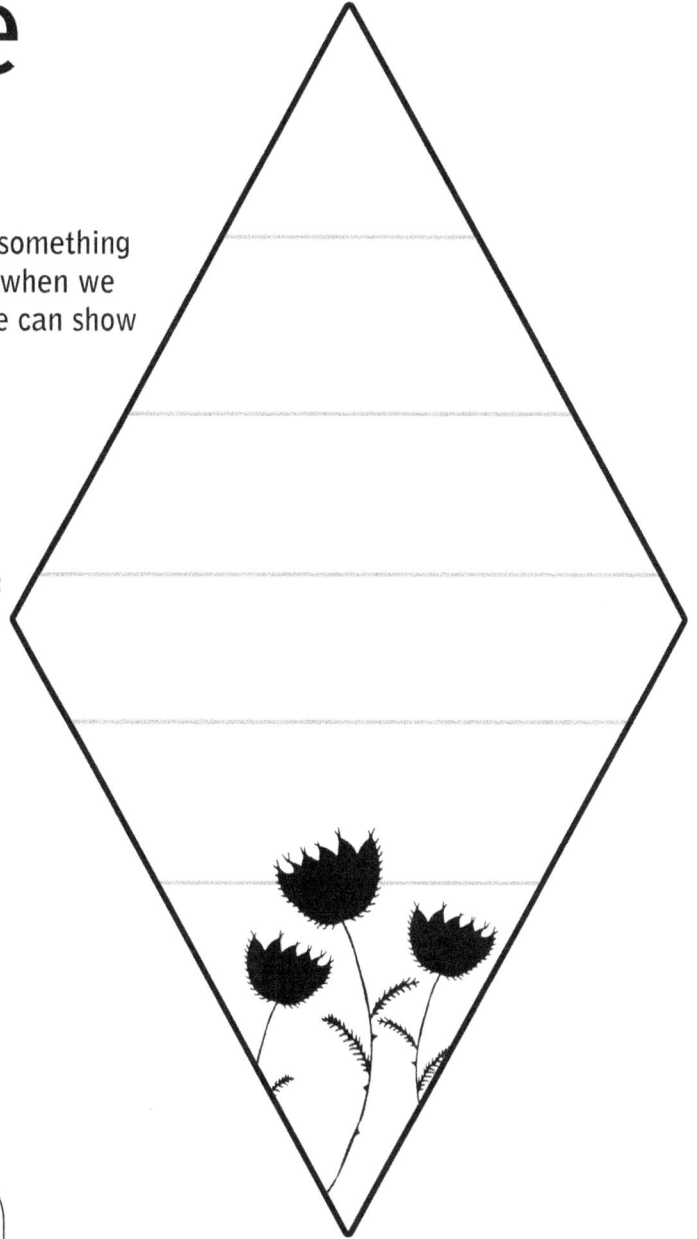

Colouring page: See page 93

Talk about the drawing:

Why is Aisha being patient in training her new cat?

What would happen if she wasn't patient and did not take the time to train her cat?

Can you think of other things that require a lot of patience?

DRAW

Draw yourself being patient

Activity 1: Trying something new

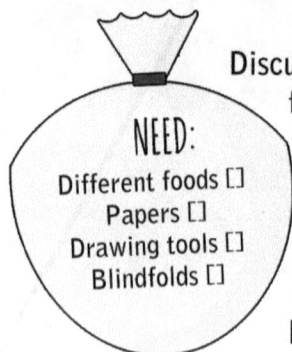

NEED:
Different foods []
Papers []
Drawing tools []
Blindfolds []

Discuss how sometimes being patient means that you have to give things a fair chance. You cannot give up on something or not try it just because you don't think you would like it.

Cut different foods (in advance) in small pieces. Vary between sweet, sour and salty foods. Have each child wear a blindfold. Give the children different foods to try. Ask them to be patient when trying something new. Have the children try to guess the foods they are tasting. At the end, have them draw the foods they liked best and discuss why we should be more patient when trying something new.

Activity 2: One drop at a time

*Suggested outdoor activity

Explain how the goal of this activity is to fill up all the containers halfway with water by squeezing the water out of sponges and into the containers. First, have everyone fill up the sponges completely and rush the process. Discuss the results.

NEED:
Different sized containers (cups, spoons, pots...) []
Small sponges []
Lots of water []

Empty the glasses and start over. This time explain how the only way to be precise is by being patient and going slowly.
Have the children start over and take their time. Help them work together to make sure everything is filled up halfway only.
Discuss the benefits and challenges of being patient.

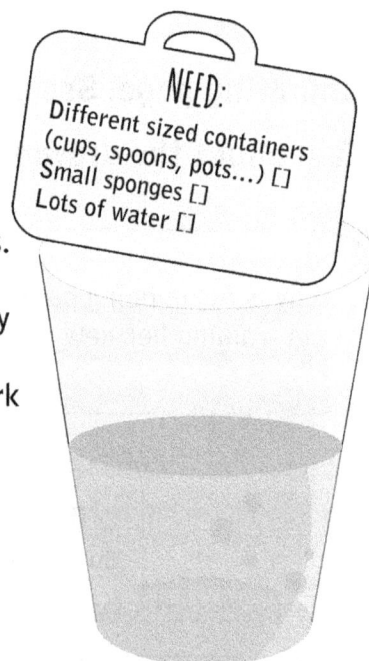

Ways to bring up Patience:

💜 Express your gratitude when children show patience.

💜 Prepare children in advance when they are going to have to show lots of patience.

💜 When doing daily activities (cooking, baking, doing laundry) talk about how you have to be patient for certain things to happen or to be enjoyed.

💜 Have a timer handy. Explain what will happen after the timer rings and what behaviour would show patience while they wait for the timer to ring.

💜 Give children some quiet time or playing alone time. This teaches patience, independence and allows children to be creative in entertaining themselves.

18. Respect

One way to explain Respect:

Respect is how we show that we care and appreciate other people and things. We are respectful towards others by being polite and behaving in a nice way towards them. We can show respect for the environment by doing our best to care for it.

A beautiful quote about Respect:

Write down a quote that you wish to memorize or remember.
If you cannot find a quote to inspire you, try coming up with your own.

Colouring page: See page 95

Talk about the drawing:

How can Tinka and Darthi show that they respect each other?

Do you have traditional clothes that you wear on special occasions or special foods that you eat?

How do you show respect?

Draw someone practicing respect for nature

Activity 1: Nature collage

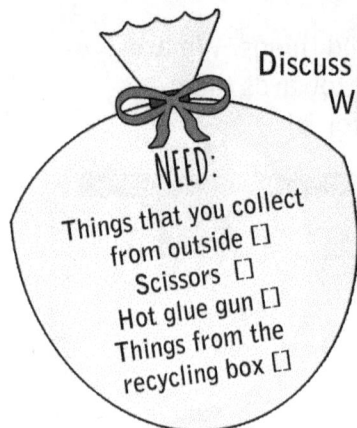

NEED:
Things that you collect from outside []
Scissors []
Hot glue gun []
Things from the recycling box []

Discuss what would happen if we stopped having respect for our world. What would happen if we started cutting down all the trees? What about if we put our garbage on the streets? Plan a little trip to a park, forest or back yard. Collect different things from the ground (twigs, fallen leaves...). Do not take anything from the trees or plants but only what is already on the ground. Gather those items together to make a nice collage or decorate something from your recycling box. Help with the use of the hot glue gun.

Activity 2: Appearances
(Participants should not help prepare or see the preparation process!)

Find 3 identical clear cups and fill them as mentioned. Make sure to stir well. Have the children look at the cups and guess the differences between the cups. Ask everyone to try to find what is different in each cup using only their sight, then using their sense of touch, hearing and smell. Finally, have them use their sense of taste.

NEED:
In 3 clear cups prepare the following:
1 cup of water []
1 cup of water with a tablespoon of salt []
1 cup of water with a tablespoon of sugar []
1 spoon for each participant []
Papers []
Drawing tools []

Once everyone has tasted everything and realized the differences, discuss how we sometimes think people are a certain way just by the way they look. When we know them better we can discover what they are like on the inside.

Draw people showing respect for each other.
Discuss how we practice respect towards each other.

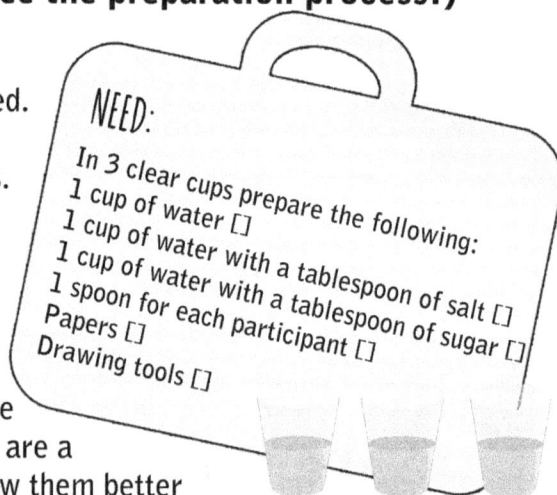

Ways to bring up Respect:

💜 Talk about being respectful towards other people.

💜 Explain that there is always a respectful way to do something. When children do something without showing proper respect, have them redo what they did with respect.

19. Responsibility

One way to explain Responsibility:

Being responsible means doing what is necessary to take care of people and things we love. When we are responsible, others know that they can trust us. We can show we are responsible by taking good care of the environment, taking proper care of our pets, being mindful of our things, and doing our best in every situation.

A beautiful quote about Responsibility:

Write down a quote that you wish to memorize or remember.
If you cannot find a quote to inspire you, try coming up with your own.

Colouring page: See page 97

Talk about the drawing:

How does Atsuko show that she can be responsible?

How do you show that you can be responsible?

Draw yourself being responsible

Activity 1: My plant

*You can combine this activity with planting a seed
or getting a new plant.

Ask the children to imagine that they are responsible for a plant.
Look at the drawings on page 59 and explain what each picture
or symbol means. Cut all the images. On a separate paper glue
ONLY the images that show different steps we do when we are responsible for a plant.
If you combine this activity with planting a seed or getting a new plant, explain what each
child will have to do in order to be responsible for the plant.
Make a drawing of a beautiful plant.

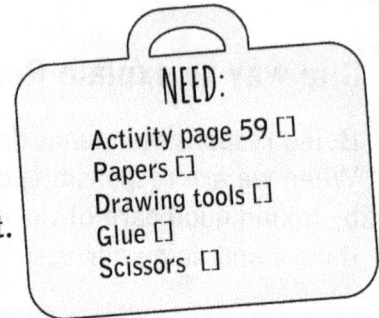

Activity 2: What happens when?

Create a character who is not responsible (make up a name) and draw
this character. Once everyone has a drawing, ask the children to imagine what
happens when this character is not being responsible by doing things like:

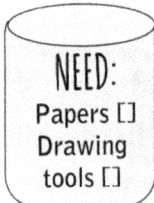

Forgetting to feed his/her turtle

Leaving his/her hat on the playground

Not eating his/her breakfast in the morning

Forgetting to tell an important message

Leaving his/her toys on the stairs

Forgetting his/her homework at school

Invent more scenarios together and come up with what would be the responsible thing to do
in each case. After talking about different scenarios, draw the character being responsible
using one of the examples you have discussed.

Ways to bring up Responsibility:

❤ Give children age appropriate responsibilities. These can be as simple as helping feed
a fish, putting napkins on the table, bringing one's dishes to the kitchen
or helping put away the laundry.

❤ Explain that being responsible is something good that comes with being more capable.

❤ Talk about why you recycle or make certain choices to be responsible for our planet.

20. Trust

One way to explain Trust:

Trust is how people know they can count on us and we can count on them. We can gain trust by keeping our promises to others. We can also show that we can be trusted by caring for others and being responsible.

A beautiful quote about Trust:

Write down a quote that you wish to memorize or remember.
If you cannot find a quote to inspire you, try coming up with your own.

Colouring page: See page 99

Talk about the drawing:

How does Tuan show that he can be trusted with the garden?

What would happen to the plants if Tuan didn't take care of them?

How can you show that you can be trusted?

DRAW

Draw someone doing something they have been trusted to do

Activity 1: Trust your partner

NEED:

Various objects to create a maze (chairs, boxes etc.) []
Blindfold []

Create a maze using various large objects around the room. Place things around to make it challenging yet not too difficult. Have areas that you have to go under or things that you have to step over. Try to vary the course as much as possible. Create a start and finish line. Blindfold one child and have another guide them through the maze. Alternate to make sure everyone gets a chance to be blindfolded and has a chance to give directions. Talk about how it felt to have to trust someone else or to be the one trusted with giving directions.

Activity 2: Trustworthiness flags

NEED:

Lots of papers []
Popsicle sticks []
Glue or tape []
Scissors []

Discuss how for others to trust us, we have to show them that we can be trusted by our actions. When people know they can trust you, you become trustworthy. Cut each paper in 2 triangles, then again in 4 more triangles (you should finish with 8 small triangles per sheet).

Create different flags by gluing or taping the triangles to the popsicle sticks. Start by having the children talk about their virtues and what they do well. Explain that each flag will represents one of these virtues. Help the children write down or draw their virtues on their flags.

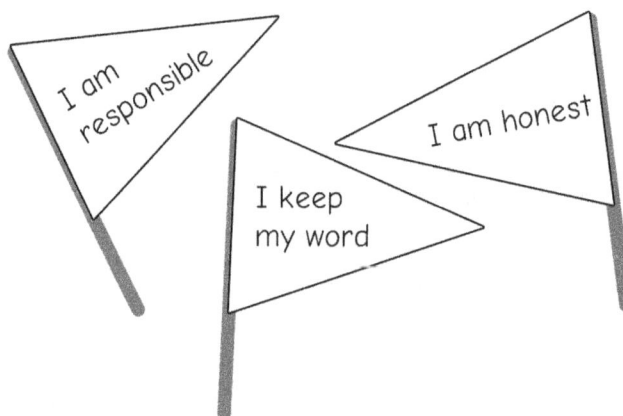

I am responsible

I keep my word

I am honest

Ways to bring up Trust:

♥ Talk about the importance of telling the truth and being trustworthy. Explain that you can gain and lose trust.

♥ Always give the benefit of the doubt.

♥ Play games in which trust is key.

♥ Talk about how every action has consequences.

THE STORY OF THE POTATO PEOPLE

In a land far away, there lived two very different kinds of potatoes. On one side of the great river lived the square potatoes. On the other side lived the triangle potatoes. Both sides were very happy. They each lived in their own houses and had their own ways of doing things. They didn't need to share anything with the other side. (Drawing #1)

One day, the great river flooded and the land of the triangle potatoes was flooded. There was so much water on their side that nothing was left of their land. The triangles quickly went in their boats and escaped to the only place where there was still dry land. They went to the land of the square potatoes. (Drawing #2)

Some of the squares were really kind and compassionate and welcomed the triangles because they knew that the triangles had lost everything. Other squares were upset. They wondered why they had to share their land and their food with the triangles. They wanted the triangles to leave. They did not care where they went as long as everything went back to the way it was. So the squares decided to have a secret meeting. (Drawing #3)

During the meeting the squares argued and argued. They could not decide what to do. Some of them wanted to welcome the triangles while others wanted them to leave.

One little square came up to the front and with a very loud voice said:

"What if the flood happened on our land?"

This little square potato asked all the squares to close their eyes and imagine how sad the triangles must have been to leave their homes behind. All the squares agreed that they would do their best to be compassionate towards the triangles and they welcomed the triangle potatoes with a big party. (Drawing #4)

THE STORY OF THE STUBBORN PIG

On a very small farm lived many different animals. The farm was so small that often the animals would bump into each other or accidentally eat each other's food. All the animals had been raised well and would always apologize when they made a mistake or forgive others for making one too. All the animals would forgive each other, except the stubborn pig. No matter how many times the animals apologized, the stubborn pig never forgave anyone.

He would say things like:

"You did it on purpose" and "If I forgive you, you'll do it again."

The stubborn pig believed he didn't need to forgive anyone because he didn't think he made any mistakes. On the day of the farmer's birthday, the animals had prepared a very special cake. They had worked very hard to make it very big and beautiful. They wanted it to be a surprise and hid the cake in a special place. The day went by and most of the animals had forgotten about the cake, even the stubborn pig. He couldn't remember if it was in the front or the back of the barn. He was getting tired and thought it may be a good idea to take a nap before the big party. The barn was very dark and just as the stubborn pig lay down, he heard a very unusual sound and seemed to be all covered with something.

"Oh no!" he shouted as he realized he was sitting on the very special cake.

He thought that maybe if he hurried he could get to the river and wash up before the others saw him, but it was too late. All the animals of the little farm stood there looking at the stubborn pig. This time he had made a big mistake.

What were they going to do?

THE STORY OF KIKA THE LITTLE BIRD

Kika was a very little bird who loved to help others, but no one would let Kika help. The other birds would say things like:

"Kika, you are far too small to help" or "How could you possibly help us, you are so tiny. We can't possibly need such a small bird."

These comments made Kika very sad and over time he stopped trying to help.

One day when it was very windy, Kika's friends were out flying. Because the wind was so strong, they were blown straight into a tree with lots of branches. There were so many branches that the birds were unable to get out. They were stuck. When the wind calmed down, they began to call for help. They shouted and shouted as loud as they could and although everyone could hear them, no one could see them because they were hidden.

The sun was setting and all the birds in the village were getting worried. They asked everyone to help find their missing friends. Everyone, except Kika. Little Kika was sad that he had not been asked to help, but he decided that his friends needed him and he was going to try his best anyway. Kika may have been small, but he could fly very fast. Kika would fly from one tree to the next and because he was so small, he managed to fly all the way through the branches. While others were caught inside the trees and branches and had to give up, Kika kept going and going. After looking very hard, Kika was able to find his friends. They were tired and hungry but very proud of their friend Kika for being so helpful and not giving up when everyone said he was too small to help.

Do you think Kika was too small to help?

What do you think Kika's friends said when they saw him?

What other lessons can we learn from Kika?

Can you make a drawing of Kika?

THE STORY OF TINY THE LITTLE PONY

For as long as he could remember Tiny was teased for being small. After all, he was just a little pony. His family had even named him Tiny and that made him feel even smaller. One day while Tiny was grazing on the farm, he saw something strange. All the hay had fallen out of the wagon and Tiny knew that it would take the farmer a very long time to put it back unless he had some help. Tiny really wanted to help. He tried pushing the hay. As hard as he tried, it would not move. Tiny tried pulling the hay. He pulled and pulled, but still it would not move. That's when Brown came. Brown was a big and strong horse.

Brown had been on the farm for a very long time and knew just how to push the hay. Brown got it right on the first try. He pulled it this way and pushed it that way, and before long all the hay was gathered in a nice pile. The farmer would be very happy when he came back.

Brown went off to the field while Tiny pushed the little pieces of hay that had fallen behind. When the farmer came out he noticed Tiny pushing the hay and thought that Tiny had done all the work by himself. Tiny had never seen the farmer so happy. That night the farmer gathered all the animals to tell them how brave and strong little Tiny was for pushing all the hay by himself.

Tiny had never felt very special and now he felt like the biggest animal on the farm. He saw Brown standing quietly in a corner. Tiny didn't know what to do.

What do you think Tiny did?

Come up with two different ways of finishing the story.

Caring

Caring

Caring

Caring

Caring

Caring

Caring

Caring

Caring

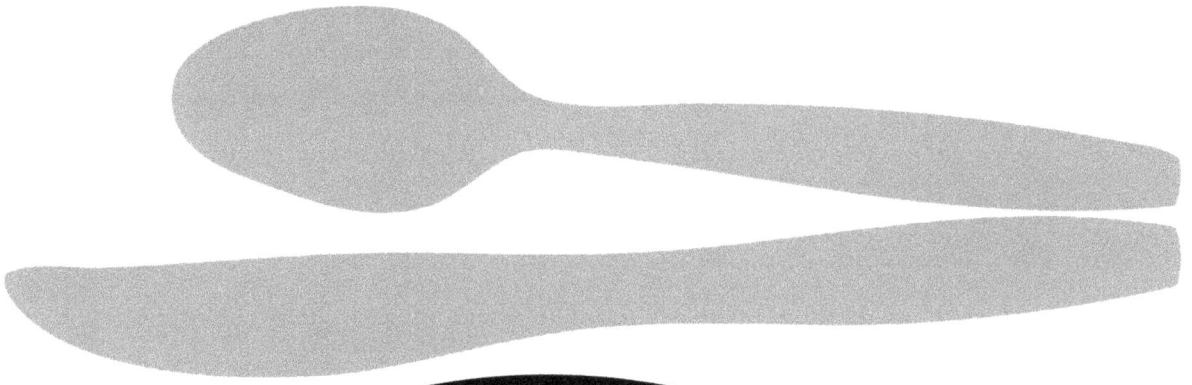

Soap

Shampoo

Towel

Teddy bear

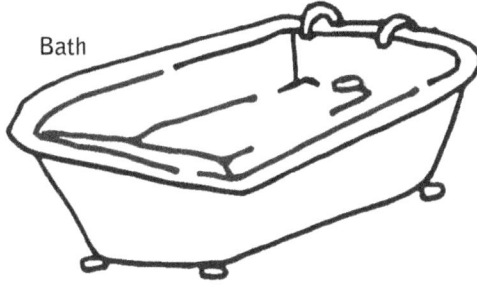

Bath

Oven mitt

Alarm clock

Tissue box

Garbage can

Hanger

Dust pan

Brush and comb

Toothbrush and toothpaste

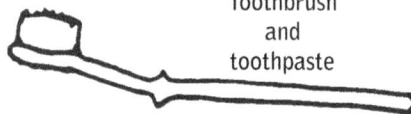

Paper tower

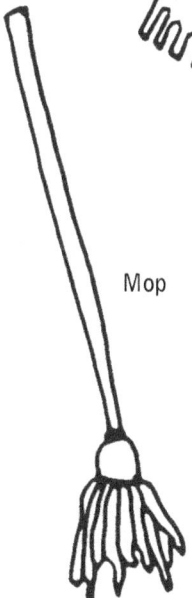

Mop

Nail clipper

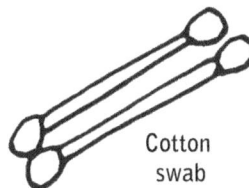

Cotton swab

Sponge

Reading a story
to someone
who cannot read

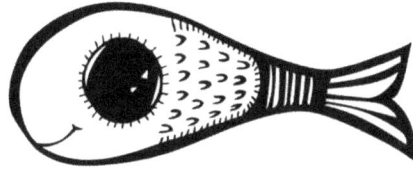

Making lots
of noise at night

Eating

Cleaning your room

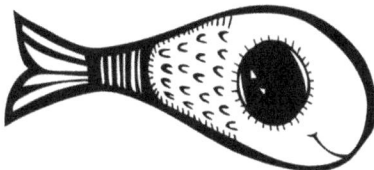

Helping to set
the table

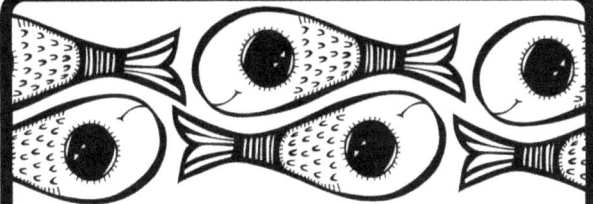

Giving your seat
to someone else

Not sharing
your toys

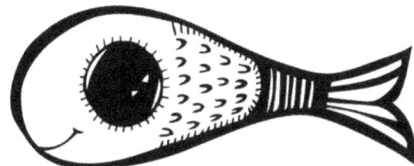

Yelling at someone
when we are
mad at them

Not helping

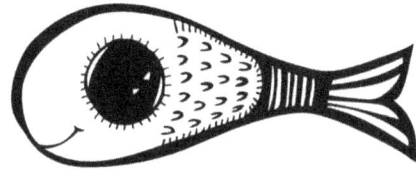

Forgiving someone
who made a mistake

Singing a song to
calm your baby
brother or sister

Hitting someone
else because
they hit you first

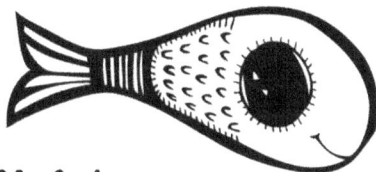

Helping your
grandmother
in the garden

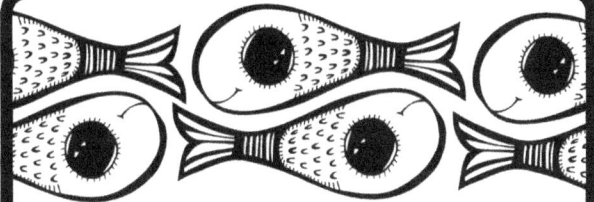

Sharing your
markers with
others

Helping a bird
that has fallen

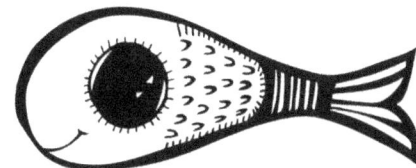

Not keeping
your promise

Go to the zoo

Add water

Tell someone you love them

Try a hat on

Go shopping

Put your plant in the sun

Find a pot

Make a big hole outside

Make new friends

Plant a seed

Help with the recycling

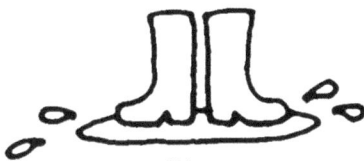
Play in the rain

Feed your baby brother or sister

Put earth and mix

Listen to music

Feed the bird

Valentine made her friend a nice card
to show how much she cared for her.

Caring

Neema and Bella always help
keep their room clean.

Cleanliness

Tom and Zara know how to cooperate,
whether they are working
on a school project or just playing.

Cooperation

Jake feels sad for Maya
because she hurt her knee.

Compassion

Basanti shows courage by walking
very far everyday to get water.

Courage

Tiko and Katinka use their creativity
to make a boat.

Creativity

Pierre shows determination
in learning a new sport.

Determination

Tom forgives Kiara for breaking his castle.
He knows that it was an accident
and that she is very sorry.

Forgiveness

Mei Lee shares her lunch with
Sheila who had nothing
in her lunch box today.

Generosity

Isaac is gentle with his new kitten
because he doesn't want to hurt it.

Gentleness

Itach helps his mother
by taking care of his baby sister.

Helpfulness

Ian tells the truth when asked
about the missing sheep.

Honesty

Maria and Aisha are best friends.
They always share their toys and are very
joyful when they play together.

Joyfulness

Wanni shows that she can be just by
sharing the pie equally with her friend.

Justice

Aiko takes care of a bird
that has fallen and hurt itself.

Kindness

To show her love, Sumie made her mom a nice
paper decoration with lots of hearts.

Love

Aisha is very patient in training her new cat.

Patience

94

Tinka and Darthi respect
each other's different cultures.

Respect

Atsuko is being responsible for the environment
by recycling paper and cans.

Responsibility

Tuan has shown that he can be trusted
to take care of the garden.
He never forgets to water the plants.

Trust